Kim's COOKBOOK

ILLUSTRATED
BY
ELLEN A. NELSON

RECIPES

SELECTED BY DORIS B. YOUNG

MEMBER OF AMERICAN HOME ECONOMICS ASSOCIATION

Manufactured and Distributed in Canada by
Regal Stationery Co. Limited
Toronto, Canada   M4G 2L6

Kim's Cookbook for Young People

THIS BOOK BELONGS TO

CONTENTS

Hi! My name is Kim!

Know what? I just found out that I'm a gourmet and it's fun. You can be one too. It's easier to be a "goor-may" than to say gourmet because it's a French word for anyone who likes to make good things to eat and drink.

All you have to do to be that word is to know how to cook and that's as much fun as eating what you make. Cooking is easy to do and there are so many fun things to make you will want to be cooking all the time.

My friends and I have made all the things you'll find in my cook book. We've made breakfast for Mom and Dad, lunches for our friends, snacks in the afternoon and all kinds of drinks for parties or when friends get together.

There are only three things to remember to be a real good cook. First, ask Mom. Then follow the easy steps very carefully and, finally clean up afterwards.

Bon appétit! That's another French word for "good eating."

Kim

KITCHEN SAFETY

1. Ask permission to use the kitchen and the ingredients.
2. Wash your hands and dry them thoroughly.
3. Turn handles of pans so they don't stick out over the edge of the stove.
4. Use pot holders when handling hot pans so you won't burn yourself.
5. Use long-handled wooden spoons when stirring food on the stove.
6. Lift the lids of saucepans or casseroles away from you so the steam will not burn you.
7. Be sure your hands are dry when you plug in or disconnect any appliance.
8. Wipe up all spills right away.
9. Be careful with sharp knives. Use a cutting board.
10. Clean up and put away all the dishes when you finish.

COOKING UTENSILS

COOKING DICTIONARY

Bake—to cook in the oven

Beat—use a brisk over-and-over motion

Boil—to cook in water hot enough to bubble

Broil—to cook under the broiler in the stove

Chop—to cut into small pieces

Cream—to beat until fluffy.

Drain—to pour off liquid from food

Fry—to cook in hot fat

Mix—to stir with a spoon or mixer

Pare—to cut away the outside skin

Saute—to cook in skillet with a small amount of fat

Stir—to mix with a round-and-round motion

Whip—to beat very fast with an egg beater

MEASUREMENTS

3 teaspoons = 1 tablespoon

4 tablespoons – 1/4 cup

1 cup = 8 ounces

2 cups = 1 pint

4 cups = 1 quart

1/2 cup butter = 1/4 pound or 1 stick

BROILED GRAPEFRUIT
(Great for a cold winter's morning)

Cut in half ——————— 1 grapefruit

With a sharp knife, cut around each section.

Sprinkle over each half ——————— 1 tblsp. brown sugar

Place under the broiler.
When the sugar is melted and the edges of the grapefruit are a light brown, remove from heat.
Garnish with a maraschino cherry.
Serve at once.

CINNAMON TOAST FINGERS

Toast ——————— 2 slices bread

Cut each into four strips.
Butter each strip.

Mix together ——————— 1 tblsp. sugar
1 tsp. cinnamon

Sprinkle cinnamon sugar on toast strips. Put under broiler until sugar melts. Serve with hot cocoa.

SCRAMBLED EGGS

Break into a small bowl ———— 2 eggs

Beat with a fork.

Add ————
2 tblsp. milk
1/4 tsp. salt
few grains pepper

Melt in frying pan ———— 1 tblsp. butter

Pour in egg mixture.
Cook slowly over low heat, scraping the cooked portions from the
bottom and sides of the pan with a spatula.
Serve while eggs are still warm, moist and glossy.

ADD-INS

To the eggs and milk you can add —
2 slices diced
American cheese

OR
2 pieces of cooked
crumbled bacon

OR
1/2 cup diced ham

For one serving.

SURPRISE MUFFINS

Set oven at 400°.

Beat ———————————— 1 egg

Add ———————————— 1 cup milk
3 tblsp. melted butter

Sift together and add ———— 2 cups flour
4 tsp. baking powder
3 tblsp. sugar
1/2 tsp. salt

Mix well, but do not beat.
Grease muffin tins.
Fill each one-third full.

Put into each hole ———————— 1/2 tsp. jelly (any kind)

Cover with remaining batter. Bake 25 minutes.

PIGS IN BLANKETS
(Good for lunches, too)

Set oven at 400°.

Open ———————————— 1 can refrigerator
biscuits

With a rolling pin, flatten out each biscuit.

Roll up in each biscuit ———— 1 brown-and-serve
sausage

Fasten with a toothpick.
Bake for 10 minutes.

COCOA
(Serve hot with your surprise muffins)

Mix in a saucepan ——————

> 3 tblsp. sugar
> 3 tblsp. cocoa
> few grains of salt

Add ——————

> 3/4 cup hot water

Boil 2 minutes, stirring constantly.

Add ——————

> 2 1/4 cups milk

Heat until the cocoa steams. Do NOT boil.

Add ——————

> 1/2 tsp. vanilla

Serve hot.

EGGNOG

Beat until stiff, but not dry ——————

> 1 egg white

In another bowl, beat ——————

> 1 egg yolk

To this—add ——————

> 1 tblsp. sugar
> 1 cup milk

Beat until well blended.

Add ——————

> 1/4 tsp. vanilla

Fold in beaten egg whites. Sprinkle nutmeg on top.
For one serving.

FLAP-JACKS

Sift into a bowl —————

1 1/2 cups flour
2 1/2 tsp. baking powder
2 tblsp. sugar
3/4 tsp. salt

In another bowl, beat —————

1 egg
1 1/4 cups milk
3 tblsp. melted butter

Pour liquid mixture into the dry ingredients, and stir just enough to mix. The batter will be lumpy.

Heat frying pan, lightly greased, until hot, but not smoking.

Spoon out 1 tblsp. batter for each pancake.

When bubbles appear on the pancakes, flip them over to brown the other side.

Serve with butter and syrup.

For variety, you may add
to the batter. —————

1 cup diced apple
or
1/2 cup blueberries
or
1/2 cup crushed pineapple
(drained)

(Serves 2 or 3)

TOMATO SOUP WITH CROUTONS

(Good for a change of pace on a cold morning)

Heat together —————— 1 can condensed tomato
soup
1 can milk

To make croutons:
Set oven at 350°.

Brush with melted butter —————— 2 slices bread

Cut into cubes.
Place on baking sheet.
Bake 15 minutes.
Sprinkle a few croutons on each serving of soup.

TOAD IN A HOLE

(A great favorite with campers)

With a round cookie cutter
make a hole in —————— 1 slice of bread

Butter both sides of the bread.

In frying pan, melt —————— 1 tblsp. butter

Place bread in frying pan.

Break into a saucer —————— 1 egg

Gently slip the egg into the hole.
Cook until firm, then turn with a spatula.
Eat while hot.

JELLY OMELET
(A French dish, good for breakfast or lunch)

Beat together

2 tblsp. milk
2 egg yolks
1/2 tsp. baking powder

In another bowl, beat until stiff

2 egg whites
1/4 tsp. salt

Fold the yolk mixture lightly into the whites.

In a frying pan, melt

1 tblsp. butter

Pour the batter into the hot frying pan.

As the omelet cooks, push back the edges, letting the liquid and foam run to the sides of the skillet.

When the omelet is set, spread it with jam or jelly.

Gently fold the omelet in half.

Sprinkle the top with powdered sugar. Serves 2

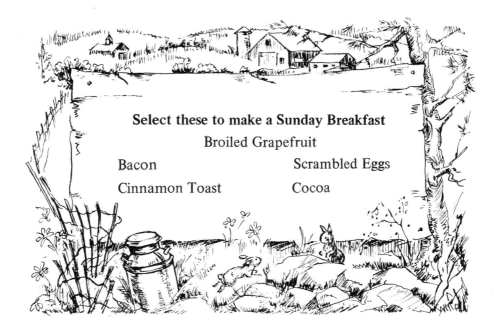

Select these to make a Sunday Breakfast
Broiled Grapefruit

Bacon   Scrambled Eggs

Cinnamon Toast   Cocoa

7

CORN CHOWDER

Saute slowly until lightly browned —— 2 tblsp. diced salt pork or bacon

Add and cook until soft —— 3 tblsp. chopped onions

Add —— 1 cup water
2 cups diced raw potatoes

Boil gently until the potatoes are tender (about 10 minutes).

Add —— 3 cups milk
1 can cream style corn

Heat.

Add —— 2 tblsp. butter

Season with salt and pepper, garnish with chopped parsley.
Makes about 6 cupfuls, but is better the next day.

MOCK PIZZA

In a food-chopper, grind together —

6 slices bacon
1/4 green pepper
2 ripe tomatoes
1/2 lb. velveta cheese
small onion

Spread on hamburger rolls or small Vienna rolls and broil until brown.

GRILLED CHEESE SANDWICH

On ——— 1 slice bread

Place ——— 1 slice American cheese

If you wish, spread on ——— 1/2 tsp. prepared mustard

Cover with ——— 1 slice bread

Brush the outside of the sandwich with melted butter. Grill in a frying pan until brown, turning once.
(For a change, try grape jelly instead of the mustard)

PEANUT BUTTER SPECIALS

Combine ————————————

1/2 cup peanut butter
1/2 cup finely chopped
raisins
Dash of salt
1 tblsp. orange juice

Spread on white or dark bread. Cut in triangles.

PEANUT BUTTER AND HONEY

Mix ————————————

1/2 cup peanut butter
2 tblsp. chopped nuts
2 tblsp. honey

Spread on bread and cut in halves.

PEANUT BUTTER AND BANANAS

Peel and mash ————————————

1 ripe banana

Mix in ————————————

1/2 cup peanut butter
1 tblsp. mayonnaise

Spread on bread and cut in halves or quarters.

CREATE YOUR OWN SOUP

In a saucepan put ——————
> 1 can condensed
>   tomato soup
> 1 can condensed
>   clam chowder
> 1 can milk

Mix well and heat slowly.
Sprinkle with crisp croutons.

OTHER GOOD COMBINATIONS

Mix and heat together ——————
> 1 can vegetable-
>   beef soup
> 1 can vegetable
>   soup
> 1 can water

OR

Mix together and heat ——————
> 1 can cream of
>   chicken soup
> 1 can vegetable-
>   beef soup
> 1 can water
> 1 can milk

INDIVIDUAL PIZZAS

Pre-heat oven to 450°

In a frying pan, brown ———— 1/2 lb. hamburg

On a piece of waxed paper, roll into
individual round circles — 1 can refrigerator biscuits

Place on buttered cookie sheet and
spread with meat.

Spoon on ———— 1 can tomato sauce

Top with ———— 1/2 cup grated cheese

Sprinkle on ———— 1 tsp. oregano

Dot with butter. Bake 8-10 minutes.

QUICK CREAMED CHICKEN

In a saucepan, heat ———— 1 can cream of
    mushroom soup
1/4 cup milk

Add ———— 1 cup cooked
    chicken
1 pimento, diced
1/4 cup chopped
    celery

Cook slowly to blend flavors. Serve on toast or rice.

STUFFED HOT DOGS

Slit lengthwise —————— 6 hot dogs

Slice 1/4 in. thick —————— 1/4 lb. cheddar cheese

Stuff each hot dog with cheese.

Wrap around hot dogs —————— 6 strips bacon

Secure at both ends with toothpicks.
Broil 10 minutes or until cheese is melted and bacon and hot dogs are brown. These may also be baked in a 450° oven for 20 minutes.

PEANUT BUTTER AND BACON CRUNCHES
(This may also be done with toast)

In a frying pan, cook —————— 2 slices bacon

Split and butter —————— 1 English muffin

Broil until golden brown.
Spread peanut butter on cooked English muffin.
Crumble bacon on top of peanut butter.

TUNA BURGERS

Set oven at 350°.

Mix together —————

1 can flaked tuna
1 cup chopped celery
1 small onion, minced
1/2 cup diced cheese
1/2 cup chopped ripe olives
1/4 cup mayonnaise
    salt and pepper

Fill —————

6 hamburger buns

Wrap each in foil.
Place on cookie sheet and bake 18-20 minutes.

SLOPPY JOE'S
(Everybody likes these)

In a frying pan, brown —————

1 lb. ground beef

Stir in —————

1 can tomato soup
1 tblsp. prepared
    mustard
1/2 tsp. salt

Simmer 10 minutes, stirring two or three times.
Spoon over warm sliced hamburger rolls.

15

HAMBURG SURPRISES

To ——————————— | 1 lb. ground beef

Add ——————————— | 1 tsp. salt
1/2 tsp. pepper

Press into eight thin patties.

Cut into quarters ——————— | 2 slices American
cheese

Place two quarters of cheese between each two patties of meat.
Squeeze the edges until sealed.
Broil 6-8 minutes on each side—or
Fry on greased griddle until brown on each side.
Serve on warm hamburger rolls.

Add-ons, if you wish ——————— | Relish
Onion slices
Catsup
Tomato slices

(Makes 4 servings)

OPEN-FACE PARTY SANDWICHES

With a round cookie cutter, cut out — | 6 circles of bread

Spread with peanut butter.
Use raisins for the eyes and mouth.
Use grated carrot for the hair.
(Fun to make for your younger brother's birthday party)

CHEESE DREAMS

For each person take ——— 1 slice bread

Put on ——— 1 slice American cheese

Add ——— 1 slice tomato

Place on the tomato ——— 1/2 slice bacon

Broil until bacon is cooked and cheese starts to melt.

WESTERN SANDWICH

In a small bowl, beat with a fork — 1 egg

Add ———
1 tblsp. water
1 tblsp. minced onion
1 slice ham or bologna, chopped

Melt in small frying pan ——— 1 tblsp. butter

Pour in egg mixture.
Cook until firm, pulling the mixture away from the edges.
Carefully turn over to brown the other side. Serve on bread or toast.
(An Eastern sandwich is without the onion)

18

CHOCOLATE MILK SHAKE

Beat until fluffy —————————

> 2 tblsp. chocolate syrup
> 1 cup cold milk
> 1 scoop chocolate
>   ice cream

Pour into a tall glass. You can substitute different flavors for the syrup and ice cream.

There are more recipes for drinks in the Snack section.

MARSHMALLOW PARFAITS

Dissolve —————————

> 1 pkg. Jell-o
>   (any flavor)

In —————————

> 1 cup boiling water

Add —————————

> 1 cup cold water

Chill until very thick.

Whip half of the gelatin until fluffy.

Into custard cups or sherbet glasses, spoon one-half of the clear gelatin.

Top with —————————

> 1 cup miniature or diced
>   marshmallows

Add whipped gelatin.

Add remaining clear gelatin.

Chill. Garnish with whipped topping. Serve.

19

BAKED CUSTARD

Turn oven to 300°

Over low heat scald ———————

| 2 cups milk |

In a bowl mix ———————

| 3 eggs |
| 4 tblsp. sugar |
| 1/8 tsp. salt |
| 1/2 tsp. vanilla |

Add hot milk gradually and stir until smooth.

Pour into buttered custard cups. Sprinkle with nutmeg.

Set in pan half filled with hot water.

Bake 30 minutes or until a knife inserted in the custard comes out clean.

(Makes 4 servings)

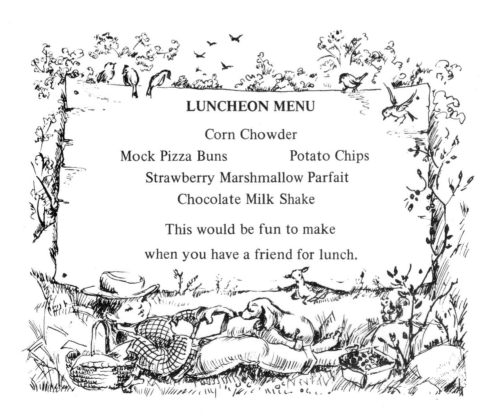

LUNCHEON MENU

Corn Chowder

Mock Pizza Buns   Potato Chips

Strawberry Marshmallow Parfait

Chocolate Milk Shake

This would be fun to make

when you have a friend for lunch.

AMERICAN CHOP SUEY

Preheat oven to 350°

Cook according to package
directions

| 1 cup macaroni |

In a frying pan heat

| 1 tblsp. oil |

Add

| 1 onion, chopped |

Cook until tender.

Add

| 1/2 lb. ground meat |

Cook until brown. Then add

| 1 can tomatoes |
| 1/2 tsp. salt |

Mix in the cooked macaroni. Put in greased casserole dish.
Top with grated cheese. Bake 25-30 minutes.

POT ROAST IN FOIL

Preheat oven to 275°

In a large piece of heavy
duty foil put

| 3-4 lb. pot roast |
| 1 envelope onion soup mix |
| 1 can cream of mushroom soup |

Seal package. Place in pan and cook for 3-4 hours. The last hour
you may add potatoes, onions and carrots if you wish.

ALMOST ITALIAN SPAGHETTI

In a frying pan heat —— 1 tblsp. oil

Add —— 1 onion, chopped

Cook until tender.

Add —— 1/2 lb. ground meat

Cook until brown. Then add ——
1 15 1/2 oz. can spaghetti
in tomato sauce
1/2 tsp. salt

Cook until heated through.

INDIVIDUAL MEAT LOAVES

Preheat oven to 350°
In a bowl beat —— 1 egg

Add and mix lightly ——
1/3 cup soft bread crumbs
1 tsp. minced onion
1 tsp. salt
1/4 tsp. pepper
3 tblsp. evaporated milk
1 lb. ground meat

Shape into four small meat loaves or put in greased muffin tins.
Spread with prepared mustard or ketchup if you wish.
Bake 20 minutes.

BARBECUED SPARERIBS

Preheat oven to 425°

Into an open roasting pan put ———— | 2 1/2 lb. fresh spareribs

Sprinkle with ————

2 tblsp. lemon juice
1 tsp. salt
1/4 tsp. pepper

Cook for 20 minutes.

While these are cooking,
mix together ————

1 tsp. salt
1 tsp. chili powder
2 cups water
1/4 cup vinegar
1/4 cup Worcestershire
    sauce
1 cup ketchup
1 tsp. celery seed
1/4 cup brown sugar

Reduce oven heat to 350°
Pour sauce over meat and bake for 1 1/2 hours. Turn spareribs over at
least once while cooking.

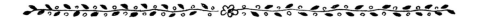

CRISPY CHICKEN

Preheat oven to 350°

Wash and dry ———— | 1 cut-up chicken or pieces

Rub all over with ———— | 1/4 cup of oil

Crush between two pieces of waxed paper 1 medium bag of potato
chips.
Roll chicken in crushed chips and bake 1 hour in an open pan.

CAN-CAN CHICKEN

In a large skillet combine ———

1 can cream of chicken
 soup
1 can cream of celery soup
1 soup can water
1 1/3 cup minute rice
1 12 oz. can chicken, cut
 up

Bring mixture to a boil. Cover and simmer seven minutes.

Serve over ———

1 can chow mein noodles

This is quick, easy and good!

CHILI CON CARNE

In a skillet put ———

1 tblsp. oil

Saute ———

1 lb. ground beef
1 onion, chopped

When meat is brown, add ———

1 can red kidney beans
1 can tomato soup
1 tblsp. chili powder
1/2 tsp. salt
1/2 tsp. pepper

Simmer 30 minutes
Serve French bread with this.

GLAZED CARROTS

Wash, pare and cut into slices —— 4-5 carrots

Cook in a small amount of salted water until tender—about
15 minutes.

Drain. Then add ——
2 tblsp. butter
2 tblsp. brown sugar
1/2 tsp. salt

Cook over low heat until the carrots are nice and shiny.
Some people call these golden coins.

BAKED POTATOES

Preheat oven to 425°
Scrub well and dry —— 1 potato per serving

Rub each potato with shortening and prick with a fork.
Bake 1 hour or until potatoes are soft.
Cut a cross in the top of each potato. Place a pat of butter in each
opening.

TOSSED SALAD

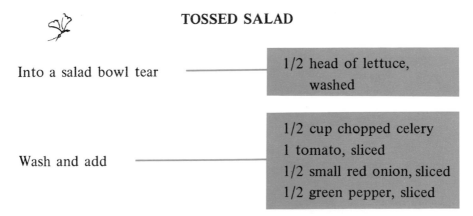

Into a salad bowl tear ——
1/2 head of lettuce,
    washed

Wash and add ——
1/2 cup chopped celery
1 tomato, sliced
1/2 small red onion, sliced
1/2 green pepper, sliced

Add dressing and toss lightly. Serve immediately.
For interest, add "Your own thing"—radishes, cheese
sticks, thin strips of ham or bologna, hard-boiled egg slices.

SIMPLE POTATO CASSEROLE

Preheat oven to 400°

Peel and slice into a greased casserole dish — 5 medium potatoes

Sprinkle with — 1 pkg. dry onion soup mix

Almost cover potatoes with water.

Sprinkle with — few grains pepper

Dot with — 2 tblsp. butter

Bake 1 1/2 hours, or until potatoes are tender.

CANDLE SALAD

On salad plates put — lettuce leaves, washed

On the lettuce put — 4 slices pineapple

Peel and cut in half crosswise — 2 bananas

Stand the bananas in the pineapple holes, rounded end up.
Press a cherry on top of each banana for the candle flame.
Serves 4

ROAST CORN

Pull husks back from corn and remove silk. Replace husks and tie ends with string. Soak in cold water for 1/2 hour. Then cook over coals, turning 2 or 3 times, for about 15 minutes.

SWISS APPLE PIE

Preheat oven to 350°

In a bowl mix together —————

> 1 egg, beaten
> 3/4 cup sugar

Add —————

> 1/2 cup flour
> 1 tsp. baking powder
> 1/4 tsp. salt
> 1 cup chopped apple
> 1/2 cup chopped nuts

Pour into greased pie plate.
Bake 25-30 minutes. Serve with whipped cream or vanilla ice cream.

CHOCOLATE COOKIE PIE

Preheat oven to 325°

Beat until frothy —————

> 3 egg whites

Add and beat until stiff —————

> 1/4 tsp. salt
> 1 tsp. baking powder
> 3/4 cup sugar

Fold in —————

> 8 Oreo cookies, crushed
> 1/2 cup chopped nuts

Pour into greased pie plate.
Bake 30 minutes. Serve with cool whip or ice cream.

TAPIOCA PUDDING

In a sauce pan mix ———————
3 tblsp. tapioca
1/3 cup sugar
1/8 tsp. salt
1 beaten egg
2 3/4 cups milk

Let stand 5 minutes—then
Bring to a full boil, stirring constantly.
Remove from heat.

Stir in ———————
3/4 tsp. vanilla

Stir once after 20 minutes.
Serve warm or chilled.
(Makes 4-5 servings)
Some people call this "fish eyes and glue", but it's GOOD.

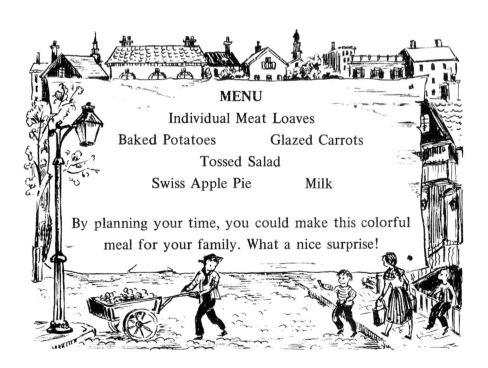

MENU
Individual Meat Loaves
Baked Potatoes   Glazed Carrots
Tossed Salad
Swiss Apple Pie   Milk

By planning your time, you could make this colorful
meal for your family. What a nice surprise!

STUFFED CELERY

Clean, wash and dry ——————— | 3 stalks celery |

Fill with ——————— | Cream cheese
Or
cheese spread
Or
peanut butter |

These are good snacks if you are weight-watching.

BAKED CRACKERS AND CHEESE

Set oven at 300°

On ——————— | 6 saltines |

Place ——————— | slices of cheddar cheese |

Garnish with ——————— | paprika |

Bake 5 minutes or until the cheese is melted.
Great with soup.

WHOOPEE PIES

Preheat oven to 350°

Beat together ——————

> 6 tblsp. shortening
> 1 cup sugar
> 1 egg

Add ——————

> 1 cup milk

Mix together and add ——————

> 2 cups flour
> 6 heaping tblsp. cocoa
> 1 1/2 tsp. soda
> 1 tsp. salt

Add ——————

> 1 tsp. vanilla

Drop by tablespoonfuls on an ungreased cookie sheet and bake
10 minutes.
Make sandwiches with this filling

Beat until fluffy ——————

> 3/4 cup shortening
> 3/4 cup sifted
>   confectioners sugar
> 6 tblsp. marshmallow
>   fluff
> 1 tsp. vanilla
> dash of salt

These are a special treat.

NO-BAKE FUDGE COOKIES

Mix together in a heavy saucepan —

2 heaping tblsp. cocoa
1/2 stick margarine
1 cup sugar
1 cup plus
1 tblsp. milk

Bring to a boil and boil for one minute.

Remove from burner and add —

1 1/2 cups quick oatmeal
1/4 cup peanut butter
1 tsp. vanilla

Stir. Drop on wax paper until cool.

TOFFEE SQUARES

Preheat oven to 350°

Mix together —

1 cup butter or margarine
1 cup brown sugar
1 egg yolk
2 cups flour
1 tsp. vanilla
1/4 tsp. salt

Press onto cookie sheet.
Bake 10-12 minutes. While this is baking

Melt in double boiler —

1 pkg. chocolate bits

Frost squares with chocolate. Top with finely chopped walnut meats.
Cut into squares.

CHOCOLATE CHIP COOKIES

Preheat oven to 375°

Beat until creamy

> 1/2 cup shortening
> 6 tblsp. sugar
> 6 tblsp. brown sugar
> 1/2 tsp. vanilla
> 1/4 tsp. water

Beat in

> 1 egg

Sift together and add

> 1 cup plus 2 tblsp.
>   sifted flour
> 1/2 tsp. baking soda
> 1/2 tsp. salt

Beat well. Stir in

> 1 cup chocolate bits
> 1/2 cup chopped walnuts

Drop by rounded half-teaspoonfuls onto a greased cookie sheet.
Bake 10-12 minutes.

These are everybody's favorite!

CHINESE CANDY

Melt in top part of double boiler

> 1 pkg. butterscotch bits
> 1 tblsp. peanut butter

When melted mix in

> 1 can chow mein noodles
> 1 cup chopped nuts

Drop by teaspoonfuls onto a piece of foil to harden.

OLD-FASHIONED OATMEAL COOKIES

Preheat oven to 350°

Beat until creamy ———————

3/4 cup shortening
1 cup firmly packed brown sugar
1/2 cup sugar
1 egg
1/4 cup water
1 tsp. vanilla

Sift together and add ———————

1 cup sifted flour
1 tsp. salt
1/2 tsp. soda

Stir in ———————

3 cups rolled oats, uncooked

Drop by teaspoonfuls onto greased cookie sheet.
Bake 12-15 minutes.

COCONUT DREAMS

Trim crusts off ———————

6 slices white bread

Cut into 1″ squares.

Pour into a bowl ———————

1 can sweetened condensed milk

Put in another bowl ———————

3/4 cup shredded coconut

Dip the bread squares first in the milk and then in the coconut.
Place on a cookie sheet and broil about 4″ from the heat.
When golden brown, remove to a rack to cool.

SUGAR COOKIES

Preheat oven to 375°

Beat until creamy —————

> 1/2 cup shortening
> 1 cup sugar

Add —————

> 1 egg
> 1 tsp. vanilla

Sift together and add —————

> 2 cups flour
> 1/2 tsp. baking powder
> 1/4 tsp. salt

Mix until well blended. Chill the dough for 1 hour.
Roll 1/4″ thick on a lightly floured board. Cut into shapes with
floured cookie-cutter. Place on lightly greased cookie sheet.
Bake 8-10 minutes.

These may be decorated for special occasions.

LEMON WHIPPERSNAPS

Preheat oven to 350°

Mix together —————

> 1 pkg. Lemon Cake Mix
> 2 cups Cool Whip
> 1 egg

Drop by teaspoonfuls into —————

> 1/2 cup confectioners
>   sugar

Roll until coated.
Place 1 1/2″ apart on cookie sheet.
Bake 10-15 minutes. Remove from pan. Cool.

SMASH-UM-FORGET-UM COOKIES

Preheat oven to 350°

Mix together ——————

1/2 cup corn syrup

1/2 cup brown sugar

1 cup crunchy peanut butter

4 cups corn flakes

Roll into balls.

Squash on cookie sheet.

Put in oven.

Turn off oven and leave cookies for five minutes.

PEANUT CLUSTERS

Melt in top part of double boiler — 8 oz. chocolate bits

Remove from heat.

Add ——————— 1/2 lb. roasted Spanish peanuts

Stir well.

Cover a plate with waxed paper.

Drop a teaspoonful of mixture onto waxed paper.

Place in refrigerator to chill.

Keep in cool place.

CRUNCHY CHOCOLATE CHEWIES

Melt in top part of double boiler
> 1 pkg. chocolate chips
> 1/2 cup crunchy
> peanut butter

In a large bowl mix
> 2 cups crisp rice cereal
> 1/2 cup raisins

Pour chocolate—peanut butter mixture over cereal.
Stir.
When well mixed, drop by teaspoonfuls onto waxed paper.

SOME MORES

On a cookie sheet place
> 1 graham cracker

Top each cracker with
> 1 large marshmallow

Put under broiler for 1 or 2 minutes or until marshmallow is
golden brown.

Remove from oven and on marshmallow put
> 1/2 chocolate candy bar

Cover with another graham cracker, mashing crackers together and
pushing marshmallow to the edges.
Try these with the marshmallows roasted over an open fire!

SAUCEPAN BROWNIES

Preheat oven to 350°

In a saucepan melt	1/3 cup shortening 2 squares unsweetened chocolate
Cool. Beat in	1 cup sugar 1/2 tsp. vanilla
Add one at a time	2 eggs
Add	3/4 cup sifted flour 1/4 tsp. salt
Add	1/2 cup broken nut meats

Turn into well-greased 8″ × 8″ square pan.

Bake 25-30 minutes.

These are yummy with vanilla ice-cream on top.

FORGOTTEN COOKIES

Preheat oven to 350°

Beat until creamy ——————

| 2 egg whites |

Gradually add ——————

| 2/3 cup sugar |

Beat until very stiff.

Stir in gently ——————

| 1 bag chocolate chips |
| 1 tsp. vanilla |

Drop by teaspoonfuls on a foil-lined cookie sheet.
Place in oven. Shut oven off immediately and do not open door
until morning!
You may substitute M & M's for the chocolate chips.
(40-45 cookies)

NEVER-FAIL FUDGE

In a saucepan melt ——————

| 4 cups miniature marshmallows |
| 2/3 cup evaporated milk |
| 1/4 cup butter |
| 1 1/4 cups sugar |
| 1 12 oz. pkg. chocolate bits |
| 1/4 tsp. salt |

Then add ——————

| 1 tsp. vanilla |
| 1/2 cup chopped nuts |

Pour into a greased 8″ X 8″ pan. Cut when cool.

STRAWBERRY CANDY

Mix together

1 cup sweetened condensed milk
1 1/2 pkg. strawberry gelatin
1 3 oz. pkg. fine coconut
1 tsp. vanilla
Few drops red food coloring
1/2 cup finely chopped walnuts

Place in refrigerator for about 3 hours.
Mold into berry shapes.

Roll in

1/2 cup strawberry gelatin

Stick green toothpicks in for stems. Add green frosting leaves if you are clever. Store in the refrigerator.

PEANUT BRITTLE

In a heavy pan over low heat mix

2 cups sugar
pinch of salt

Stir with a wooden spoon until sugar is melted and lightly brown.

Remove from heat. Add

1/2 tsp. baking soda
1 1/4 cups shelled peanuts

Pour onto well-greased cookie sheet. Break into pieces when cold.

LOLLYPOPS

In a saucepan combine

> 2 cups sugar
> 2/3 cup light corn syrup
> 1 cup water
> few grains salt

Stir until the mixture boils. Then cook without stirring until mixture reaches 310° or until the syrup spins a brittle thread when dripped from a spoon.

Quickly stir in

> 1/4 tsp. flavoring
> few drops food coloring

Working quickly, drop by tablespoonfuls on a cookie sheet and press in a stick or toothpick about one-third of the way into each lollypop while still hot.
Loosen as soon as they are firm.

POPCORN

Heat in a pan with a cover

> 2 tblsp. cooking oil

When oil looks wavy, pour in

> 1/2 cup corn kernels

Cover and gently shake pan back and forth until corn stops popping.

Melt over low heat

> 1/2 stick butter

Place popcorn in bowl and pour butter over it.
Sprinkle with salt.

ICE CREAM CLOWNS

On dessert plates place — 1 scoop vanilla ice cream

Top each ice cream ball with — 1 sugar cone

For eyes place — 2 chocolate bits

For mouth use — 3 raisins

For the nose — 1 maraschino cherry

Put whipped cream around the clown for his neck ruffle.

These are fun for a birthday party!

ICE CREAM PIE

Bake according to package directions

or use — 1 pie shell
1 graham cracker pie shell

Blend in a bowl — 1 pt. strawberry ice cream
1 cup milk

Add and beat until mixed — 1 pkg. Instant Strawberry
Pudding

Pour into pie shell. Let stand in the refrigerator 1 hour before
serving.

WACKY CAKE

Preheat oven to 350°

Sift into an ungreased square
cake pan

1 1/2 cups flour
1 cup sugar
1 tsp. baking soda
1 tsp. salt
3 tblsp. cocoa

Make 3 holes.

Into one put — 1 tsp. vanilla

Into another put — 1 tblsp. vinegar

Into another put — 5 tblsp. oil

Over all pour — 1 cup water

Mix well in pan.
Bake 30 minutes.
Cut and serve this from the pan.

POPSICLES

To ——————————— | 1 pkg. flavored gelatin
1 pkg. Kool-Aid

Add ——————————— | 2 cups boiling water

Stir until dissolved.

Then add ——————————— | 2 cups cold water

Pour into paper cups and place in the freezing compartment.
When mushy stick in plastic spoons or sticks. When frozen tear off
the cups to eat.

ORANGE CREAM FROST

Whip or blend until frosty ——————————— | 1 can frozen orange juice
1 pint vanilla ice cream

FUDGICLES

In a saucepan cook to boiling ——————————— | 1 pkg. chocolate pudding
1/2 cup sugar
3 1/2 cups milk

Cool. Add ——————————— | 1/2 tsp. vanilla

Pour into paper cups. Place in freezer. When mushy stick in plastic
spoons or popsicle sticks.

BANANA SHAKE

Peel and mash with a fork ————— 1 ripe banana

Add ——————— 1 cup cold milk
1/2 tsp. vanilla

Beat until well mixed. Pour into tall glass.

On the top float ————— 1 scoop vanilla ice cream

BLACK COW

Into two tall glasses put ————— 2 scoops vanilla ice cream

Slowly fill the glasses with ———— root beer

MOCHA MILK SHAKE

Mix until frosty ————— 1 cup cold milk
2 tsp. instant coffee
1/2 pint chocolate ice
cream

INDEX